Cornerstones of Freedom

Alcatraz

LINDA GEORGE

CHILDREN'S PRESS®
A Division of Grolier Publishing
New York • London • Hong Kong • Sydney
Danbury, Connecticut

Visit Children's Press on the Internet at:
http://publishing.grolier.com

Library of Congress Cataloging-in-Publication Data

George, Linda.
    Alcatraz / Linda George.
      p. cm.—(Cornerstones of freedom)
    Includes index.
    Summary: Relates the history of the notorious prison in San
Francisco Bay, tells about its most infamous inmates, and describes
its present-day status as part of the Golden Gate Recreation Area.
    ISBN: 0-516-20949-3 (lib. bdg.)   0-516-26349-8 (pbk.)
    1. United States Penitentiary, Alcatraz Island, California—Juvenile
literature. [1. Alcatraz Island (Calif.)] I. Title. II. Series.
HV9474.A4G45   1998
365'.979461—dc21
                                                    97-26582
                                                       CIP
                                                        AC

©1998 Children's Press®, a Division of Grolier Publishing Co., Inc.
All rights reserved. Published simultaneously in Canada.
Printed in the United States of America.
1 2 3 4 5 6 7 8 9 10 R 07 06 05 04 03 02 01 00 99 98

*I*sla de los Alcatraces. Island of the Pelicans. The Rock.

A chunk of sandstone in San Francisco Bay has been known by many names while serving as home to thousands of soldiers and prisoners. Over the space of a hundred years, it changed from an island inhabited only by pelicans to the most feared and hated prison in the United States.

Inmates called it the Tomb of the Living Dead. Alcatraz.

The island on which Alcatraz was built has become a well-known historical landmark.

Since the founding of the United States in 1776, society has wondered what to do with criminals who break the law. Throughout U.S. history, some people have believed that law-breakers should be treated harshly. Other people have argued that criminals should get a second chance—education instead of prison sentences. The debate has raged for more than two centuries.

Alcatraz became famous as one of the toughest and most secure prisons in the country. Now an important historical landmark, the story of Alcatraz helps us to understand the United States because it demonstrates how this country punishes criminals.

This map of San Francisco, California, illustrates Alcatraz Island's isolated location in San Francisco Bay.

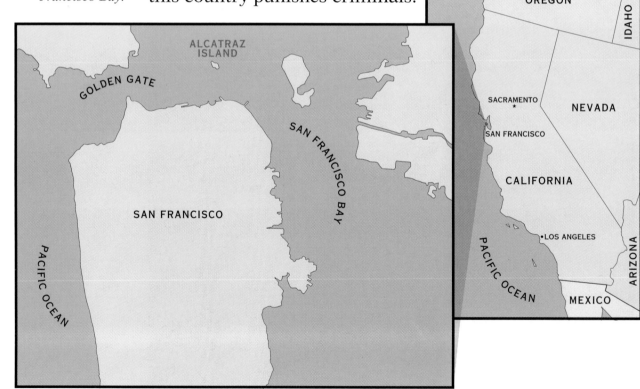

And understanding how we treat lawbreakers helps us to understand our democracy.

In 1775, a Spanish explorer, Juan Manuel de Ayala, named the island for the pelicans he found living there. Only 22 acres (9 hectares) in size, the island offered no practical use to anyone—except the United States military. In 1853, a fort was built there to defend the new state of California (which was admitted to the Union in 1850) and the growing city of San Francisco.

A two-story lighthouse was constructed on the island to guide ships into the harbor. Frequent storms raged into the bay from the Pacific Ocean through the "Golden Gate"—the entrance to the harbor.

One of the first structures to be built on the island was a two-story lighthouse.

Life was miserable for the workers who had to be ferried to the island from San Francisco every day. Only a quarter of a mile long (.5 kilometers) and 500 feet (150 meters) wide, the island had no drinkable water. The sandstone, cracked and weathered, chipped easily. With little soil, few plants could grow.

The first building on the island was the guardhouse, which was constructed in 1857. By 1861, when the Civil War began, 124 guns had been installed. Storehouses for gunpowder were built, along with "hot shot" furnaces for heating cannonballs. These cannonballs could easily cause a wooden warship to burn.

Barracks large enough to house one hundred soldiers were constructed in 1857. With walls

Today, the guardhouse still stands as a reminder of the island's famous past.

2 feet (1 m) thick, these barracks were called The Citadel, a place where soldiers could be safe during an attack. The Citadel contained enough food, water, and ammunition for many days. Surrounded by a dry moat, the only way in or out was by way of two drawbridges (bridges that can be raised or lowered). But no one ever attacked the island.

Barracks were constructed to protect soldiers from attack, but with no natural resources, no one considered the island worth attacking.

The first recorded deaths on Alcatraz occurred in 1857. Seven thousand cubic yards (5,600 cubic meters) of rock collapsed onto the roadway between the wharf and the guardhouse, burying a team of laborers. Two men and a mule were killed.

In December 1859, the first soldiers—the Third Artillery of Company H—arrived. Living conditions were poor. The post still lacked stoves and bunks. The wind blew constantly, filling everything with sand and dust. Water stood in stagnant pools on rock ledges. Construction debris littered the island. Seagulls, many of which had 4-foot (1-m) wingspans, built nests everywhere.

Eleven soldiers became the first prisoners on Alcatraz. In irons, they were locked in the basement cellroom of the guardhouse. Alcatraz was not only a fort. It had also become a prison.

The "Post on Alcatraces Island" was the only fort in operation in San Francisco Bay in 1859. With rumors of civil war, more guns were installed. The biggest guns were 15-inch (37-centimeter) Rodmans. These monsters could throw a shell 3 miles (5 km). Each gun weighed nearly 60,000 pounds (27,000 kilograms).

The army's local commander on Alcatraz, Colonel Albert Sidney Johnston, had been recognized by Jefferson Davis as "the finest army soldier in the United States." Since Davis would become president of the Confederacy if the South left the Union, some people thought Johnston might allow Southern forces to capture Alcatraz. However, Johnston soundly stated, "I will defend the property of the United States with every resource at my command, and with the last drop of blood in my body."

Colonel Albert Sidney Johnston

Despite his statement, Colonel Johnston was replaced. Brigadier General Edwin V. Sumner took over on April 25, 1861—the day after a letter arrived with the news of the Confederate attack on Fort Sumter, South Carolina. The Civil War had begun.

The only serious incident on Alcatraz Island during the war (1861–1865) was the arrival of the ship *J. M. Chapman.* Supposedly on a mission to attack San Francisco, the ship and crew were captured. *Chapman* crew members spent several weeks being questioned in the

Alcatraz guardhouse. Tried and convicted of treason (plotting against the United States government,) they were sentenced to ten years in the Alcatraz prison. President Abraham Lincoln pardoned the men, and they were freed.

On August 27, 1861, Alcatraz became an official military prison. The earliest prisoners included secessionists—men in favor of the South leaving the Union. They were confined in the bare basement cellroom of the guardhouse. By 1862, so many prisoners inhabited the guardhouse that some were kept in the cannon rooms, as well.

The men slept together, head to toe, on straw mattresses laid on the stone floors of the dungeon. They had no running water or heat and practically no sanitary facilities. Lice, fleas, and bed bugs infested the prisoners' clothing and straw mattresses. The stench was terrible.

Fort Alcatraz Military Prison, as it looked about 1865

The prisoners on Alcatraz worked eight to twelve hours each day digging out the site of the Bomb Proof Barracks. Each man was shackled with 6-foot (2-m) chains attached to 24-pound (11-kg) iron balls. If any man refused to work, he was fed only bread and water and locked in a cell called a sweat box, that was hardly high enough to stand up in.

Although the old cellhouse has been renovated for modern-day visitors, iron grates still cover the upper windows.

Another prison building was built north of the guardhouse in 1863. It measured 20 feet by 50 feet (6 m by 15 m) and had three rooms. Two of the rooms were sleeping quarters and one was a kitchen. Iron grates covered the windows. This cellhouse became the first of dozens of prison structures to be built on Alcatraz.

On April 9, 1865, Robert E. Lee surrendered to Ulysses S. Grant at Appomattox Courthouse, Virginia, ending the Civil War. Guns on Alcatraz boomed in celebration. Less than a week later, Abraham Lincoln was assassinated by John Wilkes Booth at Ford's Theatre in Washington, D.C.

As a result, soldiers stationed on Alcatraz moved to San Francisco to keep order and to stop rioting. Union supporters destroyed pro-Confederate newspaper offices and dozens of fires were set in the city. Between April 17 and June 1, 1865, sixty-eight men were arrested. Thirty-nine of them were imprisoned on Alcatraz.

The end of the Civil War meant the end of Alcatraz's duties as a harbor defense post. New military technology had left Alcatraz behind. The fort became obsolete, or out of date.

The one use for Alcatraz still in demand was its ability to house hard-core prisoners. By the beginning of the 1900s, wooden stockade walls covered more than a third of Alcatraz. Almost all traces of the fort had disappeared.

As Alcatraz outgrew its role as a fort, its reputation as a place to house the most vicious criminals began.

During the next ten years, the face of Alcatraz changed completely. More cellhouse wings were built, with brick buildings replacing wooden ones. A workshop, recreation hall, small library, and a tailor shop were also added.

Soldier-prisoners arrived in great numbers from the western United States. The worst thieves, deserters, rapists, murderers, alcoholics, and escapees from other prisons were transferred to the island. Their shirts, hats, and jackets bore a large white "P" to identify them as prisoners.

Inmates left their cells at 5:00 each morning for breakfast. Afterward, the men worked until the midday meal. More work followed in the afternoons. After the evening meal, prisoners went back to their cells for the night. Life on The Rock was boring and dull.

Troublesome inmates were chained to 12-pound (5-kg) iron cannonballs that they dragged or carried. Inmates called this punishment "carrying the baby." Other forms of punishment included flogging (whipping) and branding (burning with a hot iron) inmates' hips with the letters "D" for desertion or "T" for thievery.

The years 1876 through 1900 were relatively peaceful on Alcatraz. The prison population averaged one hundred men, with sentences averaging five years. Some prisoners, though, were serving sentences of as many as twenty years for more serious crimes.

Between 1898 and 1900, Alcatraz had thirteen different commanders. In 1899, the prison population had fallen to an average of twenty-five men. Just ten months later, in 1900, the average had grown to 441. Many more soldiers were required to guard all of the inmates.

In 1907, Alcatraz ceased being a fortress and was named the U.S. Army's Pacific Branch Military Prison. Wooden buildings— dark, damp, rotting, and unsafe— became firetraps. Prisoners and guards alike feared burning to death in the aging buildings.

As a result, new buildings were constructed. A new mess hall, kitchen, library, workshops, and washhouse were added. All prisoners moved into these new buildings, called the Upper Prison. The empty Lower Prison became a laundry and work space.

Punishment changed, too. Branding and flogging had been outlawed. Instead, an iron cage in one of the cellhouses provided solitary confinement for troublesome inmates.

Soldier-guards were a common sight at Alcatraz for many years. This U.S. Army sergeant paused for this photo in 1927.

A new era had begun at Alcatraz. Other prisons had turned to the idea of rehabilitation (teaching a prisoner to be a law-abiding citizen) rather than punishment only. In 1915, Alcatraz changed its name from Pacific Branch, Military Prison, to Pacific Branch, United States Disciplinary Barracks. Inmates were assigned to the 2nd Disciplinary Battalion, which was composed of the 5th, 6th, 7th, and 8th Companies and the 2nd Disciplinary Band. The term "military convict" had been dropped. Now, prisoners were called "disciples," or people who follow the teachings of a leader. They enjoyed a fair degree of privilege during the course of their training.

Although the name "military prison" was changed to "disciplinary barracks," the ever-present prison guards were constant reminders that life on Alcatraz would not be easy.

Inmates who had difficulty being rehabilitated were still subjected to punishment. This ranged from being restricted to their cells, to solitary confinement in the dungeons below the cell-house. There, the prisoner would be chained to iron rings attached to the floor. Kept in total darkness, they were given only bread and water. Men could not be kept in these cells for more than fourteen days. In all but a few cases, it proved to be quite enough.

The Great Depression began in October 1929, when the stock market crashed and most of the people in the nation could barely afford food, clothing, or places to live. Practically the only "rich" people left were gangsters and criminals such as Al Capone.

In this 1930 photograph, volunteers hand out free bread and coffee to the jobless at St. Peter's Mission in New York City.

Banks that were still in operation were robbed at the rate of two a day. Bank robbers, armed with machine guns, stole what little money remained. Oddly enough, some of these gangsters became folk heroes. Stories about them helped people take their minds off of their extreme poverty.

But John Dillinger, Frank Nash, Charles "Pretty Boy" Floyd, Bonnie Parker and Clyde Barrow, and George "Baby Face" Nelson were never folk heroes to the Federal Bureau of Investigation (FBI). They were known as public enemies. FBI Director J. Edgar Hoover called these gangsters "public rats," "slime," and "scum."

The government was looking for a way to stop crime. U.S. Attorney General Homer S.

Below: The FBI "Wanted" poster for Lester M. Gillis, also known as George "Baby Face" Nelson Below, right: In this photo taken at their hideout, Bonnie Parker jokingly steals Clyde Barrow's revolver. However, Bonnie and Clyde were notorious killer-bandits of the 1930s.

Cummings announced on a radio program on October 12, 1933:

"For some time I have desired to obtain a place of confinement to which could be sent our more dangerous criminals. . . . Such a place has been found. . . . We have obtained the use of Alcatraz Prison, located on [an] island in San Francisco Bay, more than a mile from shore. The current is swift and escapes are practically impossible. Here may be isolated the criminals of the vicious . . . type."

On August 20, 1934, Attorney General Homer S. Cummings inspected Alcatraz in anticipation of its opening as a federal prison.

UNITED STATES
PENITENTIARY
ALCATRAZ ISLAND AREA 12 ACRES
1½ MILES TO TRANSPORT DOCK
ONLY GOVERNMENT BOATS PERMITTED
OTHERS MUST KEEP OFF 200 YARDS
NO ONE ALLOWED ASHORE
WITHOUT A PASS

   In August 1934, Alcatraz opened as a U.S. government prison. It was equipped with six guard towers for observing every square foot of the island, barbed-wire barriers on the shorelines, and three-door security systems in the cellhouses. Alcatraz boasted the strictest security of any prison in the nation. James A. Johnston was selected to be the prison warden.

   Johnston made suggestions to strengthen the facility. The old cells were torn out and replaced with tool-proof steel that the prisoners couldn't break through. Six hundred one-man cells, built into three-tiered cell blocks, measured a mere 4 feet by 8 feet (1m by 2 m). The cells contained a fold-up bunk that was hooked to the wall, a fold-up table and chair, one shelf, a wash basin and toilet (with no seat), and a shaded ceiling light.

Most of the time, prisoners were not allowed to speak. Each day, they were allowed only three minutes during an exercise period to talk to other inmates. They were allowed to talk for one hour each weekend. Called the Code of Silence, it was relaxed after six years following an incident in which the inmates started talking during a meal and refused to be silenced.

Left: Each cell contained only the bare essentials to fill prisoners' needs. Below: The three-tiered cell blocks of Alcatraz overlapped each other to keep prisoners from climbing onto other levels.

Cellblock D provided solitary confinement and included The Hole. The Hole was a series of smaller cells with solid steel walls, floors, and doors. No light could enter these bare cells. Inmates lived in complete darkness except during meals, when the lights were turned on for twenty minutes. The maximum time a prisoner could be kept in The Hole was nineteen days.

To keep his mind occupied in The Hole, a prisoner named Jim Quillen played a game in which he tore a button from his uniform and

This photograph, taken in 1941, is one of the first pictures ever released of the row of solitary confinement cells called The Hole. Note the solid sliding doors, which blocked out all light.

pitched it into the air. Then he turned around three times and dropped to his hands and knees to search for the button. According to Quillen, "The sole purpose [of Alcatraz] was to degrade, deprive, humiliate, and break the inmates physically, mentally, and spiritually, if possible."

One of the first inmates to arrive at the new facility was Al Capone, a famous gangster considered to be beyond rehabilitation. Capone had been sentenced to ten years in prison for not paying income taxes. When Alcatraz opened in 1934, Al Capone was sent there from a prison in Atlanta, Georgia. On The Rock, Capone became prisoner number 85, and he received no more privilege than any other inmate.

Several times while Al Capone was at Alcatraz, other inmates staged protests against the strict prison rules. Capone knew he would serve additional time if he participated in these protests. He usually asked to be returned to his cell until the dispute was resolved. Because of Capone's refusal to participate, other inmates hated him and there were several attempts to kill him.

Al Capone

A prisoner could earn ten days credit on his sentence for every forty days of good behavior. Capone became a model prisoner and served only seven years and five months of his ten-year sentence.

Other famous inmates, such as Arthur "Doc" Barker, George "Machine Gun" Kelly, Albert Bates, Harvey Bailey, and Roy Gardner followed Capone's lead and avoided prison revolts. Like Capone, they all were despised by other prisoners.

Eventually, Capone left Alcatraz when prison doctors realized he suffered from the last stages of a deadly disease called syphilis. January 6, 1939, was Capone's last day on Alcatraz.

Prisoners were allowed three packs of cigarettes each week. They were not allowed

Today, photos of several of Alcatraz's most infamous inmates, their crimes, and the time they spent on The Rock are on display at the prison.

INFAMOUS INMATES

George "Machine Gun" Kelly
Kidnapping
1934–1951

Al "Scarface" Capone
Tax Evasion
1934–1939

Robert Stroud "Birdman of Alcatraz"
Manslaughter, Murder
1942–1959

Meyer "Mickey" Cohen
Racketeering
1961–1962

Alvin "Creepy" Karpis
Kidnapping, Bank Robbery
1936–1962

Arthur "Doc" Barker
Kidnapping
1935–1939

"The inmates of Alcatraz were numerous as far as public enemies went."
—former Alcatraz convict, 1941–1953

radios, newspapers, or any news of the outside world. Johnston allowed prisoners to mail only one letter each week and to receive only three. Each letter was heavily censored and retyped before reaching the inmates. Only family news was allowed.

Once a month, prisoners could have two visitors for forty-five minutes. But the visitors could only be relatives or a lawyer. During the visits, guards listened to every word that was spoken, and interrupted if anything other than family news was discussed.

Above: To help pass the time, some prisoners played card games through the bars of their cells. Right: The prison recreation yard, surrounded by high fencing and barbed-wire, where prisoners were allowed to spend a short time playing handball, softball, or sitting in the sun.

While conducting studies on birds, "The Birdman of Alcatraz" published Stroud's Digest of Diseases of Birds. *It was considered the finest work on bird diseases ever written.*

One of the most famous inmates of Alcatraz was Robert Franklin Stroud. Stroud was known as the "Birdman of Alcatraz." He had murdered two men, one of them a guard at the federal prison in Leavenworth, Kansas. Stroud spent seventeen years in Alcatraz, most of that time in solitary confinement.

Stroud's nickname came from the work he did with birds and bird diseases while in prison in Leavenworth. But officials there took away his bird privileges because of bad behavior.

Stroud was transferred from Leavenworth to Alcatraz in 1942 and confined to D Block. When Warden Johnston was replaced by Warden Ed Swope in 1948, Swope moved Stroud to the prison hospital. Few inmates ever saw Stroud again. He became "The Birdman of Alcatraz," even though he never worked with birds while on The Rock.

Poor health led to Stroud's transfer to the Federal Medical Facility in Springfield, Missouri, in 1959. Four years later, Stroud died. In spite of his fame, his death was largely ignored because he died on November 23, 1963—the day after President Kennedy was killed in Dallas, Texas.

While Alcatraz was a federal prison, there was only one escape attempt that may have been successful. In 1962, three men made dummy heads with real hair from the prison barbershop. The heads fooled guards into thinking that the

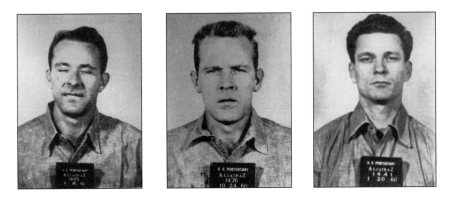

The prisoners who may have successfully escaped from Alcatraz were (left to right): Clarence Anglin, his brother John Anglin, and Frank Morris.

prisoners were sleeping, while they were actually digging tunnels out of their cells. Every night, the men explored the tunnels and air ducts of the prison, planning their escape.

Finally, the three made their break. The dummy heads were not found until the next morning. By then, the men had jumped into the cold waters of San Francisco Bay with flotation devices they made from rubber coveralls. They were presumed drowned, but their bodies were never found. A movie, *Escape From Alcatraz,* starring Clint Eastwood, was based on this famous escape.

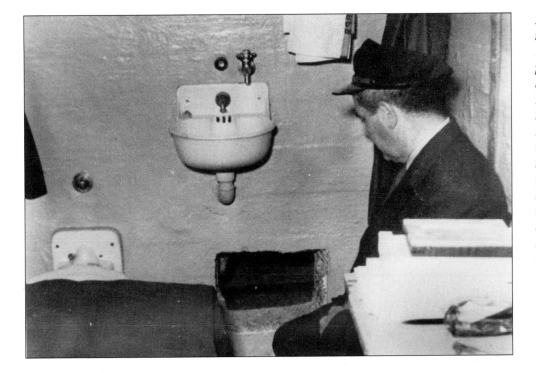

In a photograph released on June 13, 1962, an Alcatraz prison guard kneels beside the hole in Frank Morris's cell through which Morris escaped the night before. Similar holes were found in the cells of the Anglin brothers. Officials believed the prisoners dug the holes with spoons stolen from the mess hall.

For thirty years, Alcatraz remained the most dreaded prison in the United States. Stories of terrible abuse taking place there continued to reach the public. After a storm of protest, the prison was closed in 1963. The official reason was that the prison had become too costly to maintain.

More than 1,500 prisoners were kept on Alcatraz during those thirty years. Some committed suicide by climbing the walls, making them easy targets for prison guards who were ordered to shoot them. Other prisoners cut their throats with the blade from a pencil sharpener or a sharpened spoon from the mess hall. Some prisoners simply went crazy. Most prisoners, though, served their sentences without incident.

The desolation of the prison on Alcatraz Island became too much to bear for some prisoners.

On March 21, 1963, the last twenty-seven convicts marched handcuffed from the cellhouse, surrounded by news reporters with cameras to record the event. The last prisoner to leave was Frank Weatherman, a robber from Alaska. He told reporters, "All of us are glad to get off (The Rock). It's good for me and everyone. Alcatraz was never no good for nobody."

Bound in handcuffs and leg irons, the last prisoners left Alcatraz for transfer to other federal prisons. (A couple of them attempt to shield their faces from reporters' cameras.)

In November 1969, a group of American Indians occupied Alcatraz Island, claiming the land belonged to them. The U.S. government tolerated this occupation for thirteen months, and finally met some of the Indians' demands.

President Richard Nixon returned 48,000 acres (19,200 hectares) of sacred, tribal land, including Blue Lake, to the Taos Indians. (The Taos believe that Blue Lake is the source of all life.) An American-Indian university was founded near Davis, California. The occupation brought attention to the Indian plight in the United States and started a political movement to improve their lives that continues today.

Today, National Park Service rangers conduct tours of The Rock for visitors who are fascinated with the prison's history.

In 1972, the Golden Gate National Recreation Area was created and included Alcatraz. National Park Service rangers managed the island. For the first time in history, Alcatraz Island was open to the public for touring.

Today, guided tours are still offered to approximately one million visitors each year. The island, once bleak and desolate, now boasts flowers and shrubs and stunning views of San Francisco and the bay. One of the 15-inch (37-cm) Rodman cannons was reinstalled on the island, in memory of the days when Alcatraz was the mightiest fort on the Pacific coast.

Visitors disembark from a ferry at the dock where Al Capone and "Machine Gun" Kelly came onto the island for the first time. Inside the prison, the menu of the last meal served to prisoners is still posted. Visitors can see The Hole and Broadway, the inmates' name for the main cellhouse.

Alcatraz is open year round, except on Thanksgiving, Christmas, and New Year's Day. Admission is free. (There is, however, a charge to ride the ferry from San Francisco to the island.) It is suggested that visitors call ahead for tickets. Alcatraz has become one of the most popular tourist attractions in California.

From an island occupied only by seagulls and pelicans, to the most feared prison in the United States, the history of Alcatraz is linked to the history of our country. As the United States grew in population and the crime rate increased, Alcatraz came to symbolize the importance of law and order in society. The Island of the Pelicans serves as a constant reminder that our freedom is truly precious.

Ferryboats carry visitors to and from Alcatraz 362 days a year.

GLOSSARY

barracks

ammunition – things that can be fired from weapons, such as bullets and cannonballs

attorney general – the top law enforcement official in the United States

barracks – buildings that serve as sleeping quarters

Civil War – the war between the Northern (Union) and Southern (Confederate) states of the United States; fought mainly over the issue of slavery

dry moat – deep ditch dug around a building to make it difficult for enemies to reach the building

dungeon – underground prison

Federal Bureau of Investigation (FBI) – chief law enforcement agency in the United States

firetrap – building that is likely to catch on fire, or one that would be hard to escape from if it caught fire

irons – metal bands placed around a prisoner's ankles or wrists, usually attached to chains and sometimes to cannonballs, to slow prisoners down and make escape impossible; also called shackles

pardon – to release a person from punishment

sandstone – type of rock made up of sandlike grains of quartz

stagnant – foul or polluted as a result of not moving

stench – strong, unpleasant smell

wingspan – distance between the outer tips of the wings of a bird

Alcatraz was built on an island of sandstone.

TIMELINE

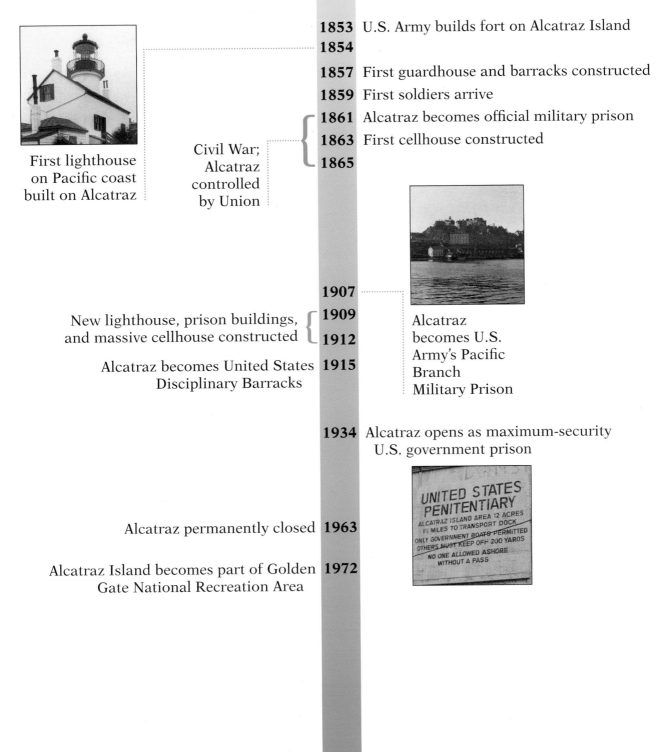

1853 U.S. Army builds fort on Alcatraz Island

1854

1857 First guardhouse and barracks constructed

1859 First soldiers arrive

1861 Alcatraz becomes official military prison

1863 First cellhouse constructed

1865

First lighthouse on Pacific coast built on Alcatraz

Civil War; Alcatraz controlled by Union

1907

New lighthouse, prison buildings, and massive cellhouse constructed

1909

1912

Alcatraz becomes United States Disciplinary Barracks

1915

Alcatraz becomes U.S. Army's Pacific Branch Military Prison

1934 Alcatraz opens as maximum-security U.S. government prison

Alcatraz permanently closed **1963**

Alcatraz Island becomes part of Golden Gate National Recreation Area **1972**

INDEX *(Boldface page numbers indicate illustrations.)*

Alcatraz Island, **4,** 8, 27, 28
barracks, 6, 7, **7**
Barrow, Clyde, 16, **16**
Birdman of Alcatraz. *See* Stroud, Robert Franklin
Blue Lake, 27
branding, 12, 13
Capone, Al, 15, 21, **21,** 22, 28
Cellblock D. *See* solitary confinement
cellhouse, 10, **10,** 12, 15, 26, 28
Citadel, The. *See* barracks
Civil War, 6, 8, 10, 11
Code of Silence, 19
Cummings, Homer S., 16–17, **17**
Davis, Jefferson, 8
Escape from Alcatraz, 25
flogging, 12, 13
Fort Alcatraz Military Prison, **9**
Gillis, Lester. *See* Nelson, George "Baby Face"

Golden Gate National Recreation Area, 28
Great Depression, 15
guardhouse, 6, **6,** 7, 8, 9, 10
guards, 13, **13, 14,** 23, 24, **25,** 26
Hole, The. *See* solitary confinement
Hoover, J. Edgar, 16
Island of the Pelicans, 3, 29
J. M. Chapman, 8
Johnston, Albert Sidney, 8, **8**
Johnston, James A., 18, 23, 24
Juan Manuel de Ayala, 5
lighthouse, 5, **5**
Lincoln, Abraham, 9, 10
Nelson, George "Baby Face," 16, **16**
Pacific Branch, United States Disciplinary Barracks, 14
Parker, Bonnie, 16, **16**

prisoners, 3, 7, 9, 10, 11, 12, 13, 14, 18, 19, 20, 22, 23, 25, 26, 28
Quillen, Jim, 20, 21
rehabilitation, 14, 21
Rock, The, 3, 12, 21, 24, 26
San Francisco Bay, 3, **4,** 8, 17, 25
San Francisco, California, **4,** 5, 6, 8, 10, 28, 29
soldiers, 6, 7, 10, 12, 13, **13**
solitary confinement, 13, 15, 20, **20,** 24
Stroud, Robert Franklin, 24, **24**
Sumner, Edwin V., 8
Swope, Ed, 24
Taos Indians, 27
U.S. Army's Pacific Branch Military Prison, 13, 14
United States, 3, 4, 5, 8, 12, 26, 27, 29

PHOTO CREDITS

Photographs ©: AP/Wide World Photos: 2, 18, 20, 23 bottom, 25 bottom, 26, 27, 31 bottom right; Golden Gate National Recreation Area: 9, 31 top right (Gordon Chappell Collection), 13 (Lloyd & Helen McDonald Collection); North Wind Picture Archives: 8; Robert Fried: cover, 1, 3, 6, 7, 10, 19, 22, 28, 29, 30; Tom Mulhern Collection: 5, 11, 31 top left (I.W. Taber); UPI/Corbis-Bettmann: 14, 15, 16, 17, 21, 23 top, 24, 25 top left, 25 top center, 25 top right.

ABOUT THE AUTHOR

Linda George was born and raised in west Texas. She earned a BS degree in elementary education from the University of Texas at El Paso in 1971, taught for ten years in the elementary grades in Texas, then "retired" to write full time. She lives near Rising Star, Texas, and travels extensively with her husband, Chuck, doing research for their many writing projects, which include historical fiction.